Heaven's Not for You

The Poetry of Josh Nazarene

༄

Heaven's Not for You

The Poetry by Josh Nazarene

Edited by Donald Zirilli

Kelsay Books

ISBN 978-1-949229-03-5

Kelsay Books
Aldrich Press
www.kelsaybooks.com

This book is dedicated to Pastor Dave,
who inspired me to find my own way into the mystery.

Acknowledgments

This book is completely unauthorized and unapproved, since I can't find anyone to authorize or approve it, including and especially Josh Nazarene. The responsibility for it is mine alone, but the credit must be shared.

First, I must thank my translators: Bill Tyndale from the Greek, Geronimo Eusebius from the Italian, Ben Bede from the Hebrew, Marty Luther from the German, and Pierre Loiseleur from the French. The research for this collection also depended on people who found and posted some of the original work and/or provided their own translations, including Ted Beza, Francois du Jon, Daryl Erasmus, Robert Estienne, Al Eynsham, Larry Tomson, Giovanni Tremellio. Bill Whittingham, and John Wycliffe.

Next I must thank the commenters who came before me. Their research and analysis were indispensable to me in helping to distinguish authentic poems from copycats and decide on the most definitive and essential versions of these poems. The most important ones, who aren't anonymous, are Bart Ehrman, Helmut Koester, Burt Mack, Jim Stuart, and Guy Vermes.

Finally, I thank the angels of this book, without whose encouragement and criticism it wouldn't exist: Greg Grummer, Addie Mahmassani, Brendan McEntee, Colleen Russell, John J. Trause, Alice Twombly, and Anton Yakovlev. And of course, thank you to Josh Nazarene, whoever or whatever you are.

Contents

The Wilderness

What did you go into the wilderness to see?
A reed shaking in the wind?
A skinny white boy in a prom tuxedo?

You mourn, but no one is weeping.
You bang on your toy drum,
expecting everyone to dance,
but you're no child.
A child knows better.

If I ate nothing
you'd call me anorexic.
When you see me at the Thai place,
you accuse me of privilege.

But I'm here for contract work.
Sign my agreement, punch my clock,
and you will find rest.

The People of My Hometown

They see a red sky at night and are comforted.
They see a red sky in the morning and are afraid.
They look for signs instead of storms.

I sailed to Tunisia. I walked across a lake of salt
to buy a difficult pair of shoes.
I returned with a certificate from beauty school,
a degree in seeing, and a doctoral composition,
but I was not received
and my house was empty,
its floors swept clean.

Child

It's hard not to like a kid. You know where he's coming from.
Kid wants an ice cream. Kid wants all the toys.
The crimes a kid won't do just haven't occurred to him.

Put your sins behind you, where you can't see them.
Run forward into life, so fast your pinwheel flies apart
and every shiny facet reveals a prophecy
in a sky unclouded by memories.

Find that impulse in you to leave kids alone, and point it at
       yourself.

The Mirror

You are every cat you curse at.
Curling in close, you can see
a brief cascade of imperfection
in the baroque mesh of the iris,
a bump in the blade-shaped pupil,
as if forged by a drunken blacksmith.
You're ready to operate,
but your hands are covered with moss
from the rotting log that covers your face,
and you wonder why the larvae aren't pearls.

The Law

I'm not against the law.
The law and I have had many good times.
The law knows all the dances
and, of course, strong arms,
square meals, stories at night,
but where is the law
when the law's been fulfilled?
Tell us, prophets.

Where are the prophets?

Heaven's Not for You

If you've ever been angry at your brother,
you're a murderer.
If you've ever insulted your brother,
you're a murderer.
If you remember what your brother did to you,
Heaven's not for you.

If you look at anyone with lust,
you're an adulterer.
If you remarry,
you're an adulterer.
Heaven's not for you.

If your right eye offends you, pluck it out.
If your right hand offends you, cut it off.

Don't swear by the earth,
earth is God's footstool.
Don't swear by your head,
you can't change one hair of it.
Don't swear by Heaven,
Heaven's not for you.

Sufficient

You can't worry about your life
and care about anything else.
Life is more than meat.
A body is more than clothes.

Look at the birds, they have no laptops
or wallets, but they are fed.
You've been thinking all morning,
but you're not an inch taller.
The side-yard battalion of lilies
you don't remember planting – Calvin Klein
has no collection to compete with these.

Look at tomorrow's furrowed forehead.
Leave it alone, slouching at its desk.
Today has all the evil
you will ever need.

Treasure

When you're in pain,
put on your best clothes.
Keep looking in the mirror
until your hair is perfect.
No one else's eye will look for you.
No one else's teeth will chew your food.
Not even your left hand will sign your name.

For a moment you forget where you are,
then you feel your left cheek burning
and recognize the anger in his face.
Turn your right cheek toward him.
If he tries to take your sweater,
give him your coat, too.
If he hijacks your car,
show him how to use the GPS.

The sun rises on the evil and the good.
Rain falls on the just and the unjust.
Any jerk will love the people who love him.
Don't pile up your treasure
where moths and rust corrupt it.
Who can steal your Spring morning,
no matter how wide it is
or how loudly it sings?
What can stain the sky? Only rainclouds
and sunglasses.

Debt

A man owed money to his boss
and begged him not to be thrown into jail.
He showed pictures of his family.
The boss was moved, and forgave him his debt.

The employee went back home
and saw a poor man who owed him a hundred bucks,
and he choked this man and demanded his money,
and called the cops on him.

The boss found out.
He felt like the king idiot, pulling at the strings
of skyscrapers and expecting music,
caressing moldy airships for true love's helium.

He looked out his urban window
and wanted to send his heart among the living,
but it would be easier to ride the subway
through the eye of a needle.

The Sower

Some seeds fell on the road
and were devoured by birds.

Some seeds fell on the stones,
sprung up eagerly, and were scorched by the sun.

Some seeds fell among the thorns
and were choked to death.

Some seeds fell on good soil
and we're still talking about what great seeds they must have been.

Talent

What will you do with your talent? Will you bury it?
Will you wave it into a flag? Will you wear it beneath your slacks?
Will you stretch your talent to keep it from going stiff on the
     couch?
Will your talent save flood victims? Has your talent signed
     agreements
with foreign nations to regulate trade?

When I come back, you will walk me to your talent
and smile all over it, but I will grab it away from you
and hand it to the State Fair grand champion,
because winners will win even more,
and losers will know more losing.

Wherever the carcass lies,
the eagles will gather.
Nothing belongs to you.

Weeds in the Wheat

Barb-rooted, bee-courted, languishing in
their glorious season, planted by enemies,
they dance a ritual of summer breezes
until finally shining brighter than cash crops,
trotting out finery tailored by sun.

The weeds in the wheat are harvested, unsurprised, and find it
sensible to be segregated. It fits their feeling,
distinguished, a class apart, so refined
they almost don't mind the torch coming down.

The Latest Generation of Vipers

They bind heavy burdens grievous to be borne
on men's shoulders, but will not lift a finger.
They buy more expensive bookcases
and decorate their lapels. They love
the upper rooms at feasts
and the box seats at ball games.
Greet them as Father, Pastor, Governor, Priest.

They devour widows' houses
and for a pretense make long prayer.
They compass sea and land to make one proselyte,
and when he is made they make him twice the child of Hell that
        they are.
They are blind tour guides.
They strain at a gnat and swallow a camel.
They clean the outside of their bowls and cups.
They are whited sepulchers,
the children of silk-gloved jesters strangling prophets.
Greet them as Lawyer, Minister, Highness, Grace.

How to Go the Wrong Way

You don't even have to listen to directions.
Just follow the people who are giving them.
There's a lot of traffic, but it's moving.
The signs, though not exactly what you're looking for,
are easy to read. The sun is only in your mirror,
which you're not checking.
The road gets comfortable.
It seems to know where it's going.

The Poison

When you were poisoned, the detectives came.
They searched your house and your possessions.
They questioned your relatives and friends.
Then they brought everyone into the parlor and announced
that the poison came out of your mouth, not into it.

Loneliness

You don't understand the power of loneliness,
but in your briared seclusion
you have the shepherd's full attention.

Love wins by losing. Love is a gathering of loneliness.
Love will eventually conquer your need to be with someone else.
Love leaves her alone. Love leaves her. Love doesn't need.
Love only gives.

Blessed

Blessed are the mourners
whose empty eyes see only what they've lost,
who drag their suitcases like chains
to unintended reunions.

The underling will roll his chair
into a corner office
and drink his coffee
while it's still hot.

Blessed are the peacemakers,
for they will be negotiated,
and their details hammered out.

Blessed are you when you're reviled,
because you're in good company.

The Pearl of Great Price

Birds nesting
in a mustard seed.

Yeast hiding
in unleavened flour.

A man mortgaging
everything he owns
to buy an empty lot.

Why I Write Poems

Because you have eyes, but you don't see,
and ears, but you don't hear,
because you hear, but don't understand,
and you see, but don't perceive.

An entrepreneur gave a million dollars to a psychic
to see what you see,
a senator begged a surgeon
to hear what you hear,
but neither of them
had the poems.

Taking Orders

The first commandment is to love God
with every bird of your being, to kiss like clouds
in contrary winds, the God in you against
the God all around you, petals from new buds.

The second commandment is the same:
to love your neighbor, a man or a woman
in a window, who yells out the same river
that runs your heart's blood to fingertips.

On these two commandments hang
all the law and prophets. Every billy club
swings it out, and from the eyes of greatest love
a salty tear gas pours, and the trees, like spears,
pull revelation from the chest they wound.

Special Instructions

Take up your guns, and follow me.
Take up your suicide pacts, and follow me.
Take up your vestigial fat, take up your blood clots, and follow me.
Take up your military contractors, your fragmentation jackets,
your silent screams, your silver springs,
your cars with closed windows on summer afternoons,
take up your cyanide and follow me.

Take up your party and follow me.
Take up your public school education and follow me.
Take up your news algorithm,
your income tax, your driver's license,
your laws written in a language you can't understand,
your street signs, the camera and microphone in every computer,
take up your drones and follow me.

If you save your life, you'll lose it.
If you lose your life, you'll find it.
If you win the whole world, you won't be in it.

Shine

Don't ask for flavor.
You're the salt in this recipe.
You can't salt salt.

You're the lamp in this room.
You belong on the table.
Anywhere else is a fire hazard.

That's It

I was hungry and you gave me meat.
I was thirsty, and you gave me drink.
I was a stranger, and you took me in,
naked, and you clothed me.
I was sick and you visited me.
I was in prison, and you came to me.
Whatever you've done to the least of us,
you've done to me.

Now I will feed you, this is my body.
Drink, this is my blood.
The poor will always be with you,
but I won't.

Afterword

On an April morning in the year 2000, investment brokers found the following poem written in bright red paint on a bathroom mirror in the New York Stock Exchange:

I never knew you.

The grapes I pop into my mouth
didn't come from thorns.
I never pulled a fig from a thistle.

You built a beach house in a flood zone,
but you're no little pig:
you're a wolf in a wool sweater.

The vandal was never found, but a full twelve years later the Instagram account saulhatarsi posted a picture of a poem taped to a donkey at the Damascus Zoo. The writing, though printed and not painted, was also red. This time, the language was Hebrew. The picture went viral, usually accompanied by this translation in the U.S.:

Let the dead bury their dead.
I'll bring you to the river's edge.
Who is my mother? Who is my brother?
The answer is shaking my hand.
The suffering will continue to suffer,
but I won't be here much longer.
Come on, let's fish for each other.

These mysterious words, in their unusual location, generated millions of likes. Their anonymity sparked the curiosity of the Internet. Who wrote this poem? "saulhatarsi" claimed he was just a tourist taking a picture of something he found.

Soon afterward, but thousands of miles away, a Facebook post told the sad story of someone climbing to the top of an abandoned viaduct in New Jersey with the intention of jumping off. He changed his mind when he saw some red graffiti that simply said "I am the Google Maps, the coordinates, and the satellite."

These two posts, united only by color, captured the imagination of the Internet, and similar finds were discovered across social media, dating all the way back to the "wolf" of Wall Street.

There was no solid evidence that all these words were written by the same person. Quite the opposite, when you consider they were written in half a dozen languages and were appearing all over the world. But often the same or similar things were found written in multiple languages.

This book is an attempt to make a coherent collection from this chaos. The translators who helped me have checked the accompanying translations or have provided new ones. Some poems are a combination of different versions. In most cases, the titles were added to give a sense of a completed poem. The name of this "ghost writer" was taken from a popular piece of fan fiction written by "Mark Lyon" that located the poet in Nazareth, Pennsylvania.

As to why an anthology should be edited for someone who doesn't exist or has chosen not to be identified or published, I hope the poems themselves provide the reason.

www.ingramcontent.com/pod-product-compliance
Lightning Source LLC
LaVergne TN
LVHW091322080426
835510LV00007B/607